becoming bone

# becoming bone

## Poems on the Life
## of Celia Thaxter
## (1835–1894)

BY ANNIE BOUTELLE

The University of Arkansas Press
*Fayetteville*
2005

09  08  07  06  05     5  4  3  2  1

*Designed by Liz Lester*

⊗ The paper used in this publication meets the minimum require-
ments of the American National Standard for Permanence of Paper
for Printed Library Materials Z39.48-1984.


LIBRARY OF CONGRESS CATALOGING-IN-PUBLICATION DATA

Boutelle, Annie, 1943–
      Becoming bone : poems on the life of Celia Thaxter
   (1835-1894) / by Annie Boutelle.
         p.    cm.
      Includes bibliographical references.
      ISBN 1-55728-797-X (alk. paper)
      1. Thaxter, Celia, 1835–1894—Poetry. 2. Isles of Shoals
   (Me. and N.H.)—Poetry. 3. Women gardeners—Poetry.
   4. Women painters—Poetry. 5. Women poets—Poetry.
   I. Title.
   PS3602.O893B43    2005
   811'.6—dc22
                                          2005000614

*For Will,*
*who loves islands*

# ACKNOWLEDGMENTS

The author gratefully acknowledges the editors of the journals in which these poems first appeared:

*Beloit Poetry Journal*: "Cormorant," "Mrs. Thaxter," "Companions," "Marriage Bed"; *Green Mountains Review*: "Cold," "Goats"; *The Hudson Review*: "River," "In the Dream"; *The Larcom Review*: "Birth (Karl)," "Birth (John)," "Birth (Roland)," "Mr. Thaxter," "Bones"; *Poetry*: "Morphine," "Spirit," "Bodies 1863"; *Verse Daily*: "Marriage Bed"; *The Worcester Review*: "Midwife"; *Yankee*: "Rowing." "Bodies 1863" also appeared in *Crossing Paths*, ed. B. and M. Sternlieb, (Richmond, Mass.: Mad River Press, 2002).

For their superb professional help, I am deeply grateful to librarians at The Boston Public Library, Harvard University, The Huntington Library, The Portsmouth Athenaeum, Smith College, and Vaughn Cottage (Star Island, Isles of Shoals).

Through a Picker grant and a sabbatical, Smith College gave me priceless time.

To my poet friends who read and critiqued expertly, especially Elizabeth Alexander, Sara London, and Ellen Doré Watson, a thousand thanks.

# CONTENTS

## shell

# NOTE ON THE POEMS

These poems are spoken by Celia Thaxter (1835–94).

Thaxter grew up on the remote Isles of Shoals, off the coast of New Hampshire and Maine. She married her father's business partner when she was sixteen, and became one of the best-selling women poets of nineteenth-century America.

For historical notes and a more detailed overview of Thaxter's life, see the notes at the back of the volume.

# becoming
# bone

*rock*

*Portsmouth, New Hampshire, October 1839*

## RIVER

The schooner slips from Portsmouth and the river
widens, a snake that opens sluggish jaws
to swallow the sea, and everything slides
past—bricks, the pared spire of the church,
wharves, chimneys, terraced plots of green,
that thin woman who bends to her basket and pegs
scraps of clothing on a line, that clump of elms,
a hearse meandering on its way, the boy
with the brown cap fishing from a pier, the silver
body of his catch twitching an arc that swings
from him as everything moves past without word
or protest and the ship glides unperturbed
into a world where nothing is left but water,
air, and the uncertain space between.

## WHITE ISLAND LIGHT

Black-capped, it rears above the rock,
the squat gray house, the fragile boat.
Nothing can touch it. Its walls are thick
with salt that scars the skin, the eye; clouds
hang themselves upon it, melt to mist; tides
lap, withdraw, return like unfed dogs;
winds hurl themselves, weeping,
against its flanks. The one still thing
on a plane of shifting waters, it pins
the globe. My father's tower, unmoved,
unmoving, on a disk of tilted sea.

# GOATS

The men coil ropes and draw water,
sharpen knives, steel on steel hissing,
open the door to the calm flood

of evening light, and shamble out,
taking the knives, the ropes, the sloshed
pails of water. They shut the door

on what we will not see. Mother holds
me, arms a thicket, voice a spell
that speaks of a cradle, the shouted

curse, the spinning wheel, and drops
of startled blood. Inside it is still
as that palace, the groom slumped

next to the rigid horse, the cook
dangling his dripping spoon, the maid
shoving her face in the cat's limp fur.

They lay the skins out in the room
at the foot of the tower, fur side
down. They scatter salt on them,

and the skins sweat golden tears.

*White Island, January 1840*

COLD

Rime rings the rock:

ink freezes; wine congeals
to splintered stars;
on passing boats, men,

tied to the bows, lean
and strike the ice, jockeys
whipping their horses,

whack-whacking what
was once a wave
but clings now, builds,

and hauls boats down.
We are bound by ice.
Father heats a coin

on the stove, holds
it in his leather glove,
presses it against

the darkened glass,
and watches as heat
chases ice. Through

a penny-sized hole,
we peer at a round
and polished world

of hardening water.

# NEWS

For fifty-eight days, we know nothing
of the world. The pilot boat from Portsmouth
batters through slabs of river ice and brings
us letters, rope, tobacco, wine, a basket
from Aunt Susan with jars of jam
and pickled beans that speak of dill
and sunshine. Mother spreads strawberries
on baker's rolls, while Father reads of opium
wars and new black tea in London, Sylvester
Graham's unblocked flour, daguerrotypes,
and Queen Victoria marrying her cousin,
wearing only *items of British manufacture.*
We laugh at everything, even the opium wars,
and Oscar's face is smeared with summer's fruit.

## THAW

Swathed in warm
fog, the islands stream
toward heaven.

*White Island, May 1840*

SEEDS

First, the dry brown
crescent of the seed,
then climbing feather-

leaves and a marigold's
frantic sun. In the plot, one
yard square, I plant the color

of fire, and Mother's belly
arches full and pushes
like a moon against the dark.

# SEA-BABY

Tangled in kelp,
swimming in its warm
dim sea, the baby turns

a knee, an elbow, shoves
out a fist, and hoists
its mother's stomach

toward the stars.
Through thin lids
it sees red plush

anemones, prickled
starfish, purple mussels
clutching rock,

and through rough
air it hears
Atlantic roar.

## WHALE-OIL

In the lee of Lunging, a black
schooner anchors, and barrels leap
ashore from tipping boats. Later,
high in the tower, fifteen lamps
revolve and whale light floats
in red and golden sweeps
across a whale-tracked sea:
it touches foreheads, flukes,
flanks, eyes. It trembles
on furrowed skin.

## MIDWIFE

In her low-slung boat,
the midwife rows from Gosport.

Every few strokes, she rests
her battered oars, and stoops

to bail: she flings rainbows
to one side, then bends

and flings some more,
in a fierce spendthrift

gesture as if she knows
there will always be water.

# CHILDBED

She hums as she unpacks
her bag: knives, needles, twine,
bottles of brown liquid, jars of salve
and grease, bunches of herbs
crumbling at her touch. Her boots
are crusted thick with mud; arms
brown and bare, the muscles clear.
Father holds Oscar on his knee
and bounces—"Trot trot to Boston,
trot trot to Lynn. . . ." In the bed,
my mother's face twists
tight behind the mountain of pale
flesh that changes shape
and bulges as she screams.

     •   •   •

Blanket-wrapped, I fold Oscar in my arms
and tell him of the shouted curse,
the spinning wheel, the drops of blood.

As his breathing slows and he grunts
softly in his dreams, I hear the talk
of water on rock, the grinding cries

of outraged gulls, a bell-buoy clapper's
iron clang, and Mother's screams flung wide.

Then, somewhere in my dreams,
a fog-torn place and funneled silence.

•   •   •

Swaddled in linen bands,
you open sleep-blurred eyes
and see me hovering
there above your cradle.
Cedric, my sea-child,
our names connect us:
the curling Cs stitch
a tight curve around
our startled hearts;
and in the sea-washed
mirror of your eyes,
I find my flushed
ecstatic face.

*air*

*White Island, July 1846*

MIRAGE

All morning long, at shifting
edge of shimmering sea,

cloud-towers waver, stretch,
and shrink. Ships ride on air,

hulls tall as Boston
buildings, sails like giant

blossoms opened wide.
He arrives at noon, the Harvard

man, uncertain, stumbling
from the boat. He straightens,

shades his eyes against dazzle,
and the cloud-towers shiver

just beyond his shoulder.

# THE HARVARD MAN

His conversation swirls,
a seagull that tips
wing to alter course.

I'm led into a new
land: blue velvet seats,
shuffle of programs,
a violinist turns a wooden
peg, the brilliance of curved
brass. Dolores's ringlets
gleam *blue-black, lustrous,*
while Mr. Longfellow paces
Brattle Street and lilacs billow
sweetness into April air.

*Sehnsucht,* desire, the words
scurry toward Goethe's dream—
oranges glowing against a screen
of leaves—or Darwin's finches
raucous in the Galapagos.

I run ahead of him
and claim this land as mine.

# MAIDENHAIR

He holds the fern high, plunges
it into the shallow pan filled
with rain-barrel water—

the hair of Aphrodite,
silver in water, instantly dry—
the Romans thought it magic.

Around each furling frond,
each stem, the nimbus
glow of saints and gods,

and Aphrodite glistens
as foam falls away and water
sheets off breasts, thighs,

toes, and she rises,
surprising the dolphins,
into clear Aegean air.

## ROWING

I teach him to row.

We spin in tipsy circles, oars
digging and flailing, his brow
soaked, his boots braced
on the strut, his beard
curling tender
on the determined jaw.

When he rests, his oars
akimbo, we swivel to a slow
blurred stop.
                    And it whirls
around us: this world of cloud
and rock, the anguished
cry of gulls, the slap
of bright, indifferent waves.

*Appledore Island, September 1847*

## APPLEDORE HOUSE

All the cool morning
the island rings
to the thunk of wood
and the sweet, sure clang
of steel on iron.

On cleared land
near the bay, four stories
high, a wooden skeleton
of what will be
rises in air.

Men clamber on the thin
ribs of the roof. Gulls soar
and dive. Clouds race
behind the rooms. I see
my future reconnoitering
there, testing the planks,
the firmness of the nails,
stretching out her arms,
in the open measured
space between beams.

# TUTOR

Cedric copies:
*George Washington is come!*
*What praise is due?*

Oscar copies:
*Fame spread her wings*
*and with her trumpet blew!*

He gives me words:
*transcendental, malleable,*
*Renaissance, dyspepsia,*
*iambic, alchemy.*

In my mind, I build
an apothecary's cabinet,
and tuck each silk-wrapped
word (*abolitionist, anarchy,*
*animadversion*) into its sliding
dove-tailed drawer,
and when I take them out,
the scent of sandalwood
lingers on each finger.

*Appledore Island, October 1850*

## LAUNDRY

Stark, against a cobalt sea,
his nightgown billows.

The tail of his shirt
flaps and rises, tugging

the line, where, next to Mother's
monthly rags, my nightgown

rises white and winsome,
a shy exhalation.

# HORSESHOE CRABS

The trench cuts and wobbles to the brown
tangled heap, the stiff tails, the hinged
flap between the smooth armored head
and the spiny bottom half. *Limulus
polyphemus:* the females reach two feet
in length, "if we include the tail spike."
He turns them over, prods the twitching
legs. His stick points out the male: its first
claws heavy, tooled for grabbing, holding
on past tunneling crabs to the scooped
burrow. He stands and draws them
in his book, labeling the parts, his legs
columns planted in unstable sand.

## ROSE HIPS

Blood-rose blooms
on the clean sheet.

The trail leads back
to the place of nakedness,

shadow-grove where briars
twist and murmur of the fruit,

its taut plumped skin,
packed seeds, the prick

of needful thorns, the wide-
hipped thickening dark.

# MEMORY

What have I forgotten
from the mirage years
when I skimmed grass
and summoned fish to leap
in air and share my joy?

The day when he and Father
divided everything
they owned in common.

The island—one house
for him, one for us.
The goods—chairs, lumber,
boats, guns, brandy—laid
out on the lawn in tidy rows.
The animals—chickens flapping
in two sacks, gray sheep circling
in two pens. Even the cow.

She bellowed when they tied
ropes to her horns. Their arms
were slick with red to the elbow.
Most of the body parts
were easily divided, the carcass
being conveniently symmetrical.

But what about the head?
who got the head?
And the heart, they must
have split the heart—
two glistening chambers apiece.

# CORMORANT

Like a cormorant, sharp
head cocked back, beak
aimed at the sun, I ride
the surge of his presence
and forget the unseen
haul of all that lies
beneath the paddling feet.

## WEDDING

The dress is merino
sewn by Mother.

While Jonas Thaxter
sails to Kittery to fetch
the minister, I gather colors
— scarlet huckleberry, purple
aster, lavish goldenrod—
and the staid parlor swims
in bold prismatic light.

Tall and grave, my husband
clutches his hands behind
his back, while Mother sobs
and Oscar punches Cedric.

After the words are said,
my husband stoops to fill
the glass. He hands
it to me, the liquid slipping
back and forth in the clear
space between his fingers.

## MARRIAGE BED

We leave them,
Mother's face wine-flushed
and Father bending low
to Jonas's whispered jokes.

We close the door and step
into coldness, the first frost
of September, stars
sharp as blades.

Muskrats rustle under roots
as we walk single-file
down the path to my husband's
house, its marriage bed
shipped from Watertown
by grudging Thaxters.

It has rocked its way
to Appledore and lies now,
placid, beside nightstand
and watery mirror.

He talks of Roman marriage,
the bride's hair parted with the point
of a spear. He whispers of sacred
bread, wolf fat spread near the door,
crocus petals falling on silk sheets.

Beneath the counterpane, coarse
wool, and linen dense with starch.

. . .

Later, I will know
he called my name.

But, at the time,
at his first crisis,
"Seal," he cries,
and then again,
"my seal."

And I wonder
is he the letter, smooth,
unopened, its surface
polished, firm folds
hiding the contents;
and I, warmed wax,
yielding to the imprint?

Or does he mean the seal
whose sea-dark head breaks
sleek through blown-back
spray, and he is the rock
I spiral round, this island
with its shining crevices,
its cliffs and graveled coves?

. . .

Leaving him flopped and pale,
she crawls from the bed
with its carved leaves
and stubborn orbs of fruit.

She sets the basin on the floor,
pours water from the ewer,
and crouches, close to the stand,
to wash. On the island

of Marathonisi, Helen
crouched like this, near
a chipped basin, cloth harsh
and cold between her legs;

and he who had dared pass
judgment on Aphrodite,
he lay there, like a flounder,
hooked, reeled, gutted,

flung down on the slab—
all that was essential
filleted from him—nothing
left but flesh.

*blood*

*Watertown, Massachusetts, November 1851*

## BEETROOT

I bend and hoist them
from the packed soil, damp
clumps hanging to them. They
swing from my grasp, limp

as rabbits, as I walk
from plot to kitchen
where the cleaver severs
leaves from root, green

from red. I lean down
on the blade, pushing it
through, splitting each
grainy blood-packed heart.

They bleed on the cutting
board. Water bubbles
red around their planes
and curves.

Next day, in the chamber
pot, urine flushes
pink, and I cover
my mouth, remember

I carry a child,
its stubborn heart lodged
there, beating a red tattoo
in the clinging dark.

*Appledore Island, 24 July 1852*

SONG

The midwife's arm thrusts
between my legs. Blood, bright
as paint, spatters the sheets, calm
red stars in a white sky. A soprano
voice rises, arching high, fine
as porcelain, almost at the point
of breaking. I count the blood
spots; obsessively I count them—
fifty-three, fifty-four, fifty-six—
until there are too many left
to count. There's applause, stamping
and clapping from the hotel parlor;
and I know the voice that arches
high and almost breaks is not my own.

## BIRTH (KARL)

Blue as a skinned rabbit,

he is pulled from my body.
I am somewhere else

when it happens.
They tell me pincers

gripped his head and hauled
him out. They show me

the marks, scarlet dented
puckers on the pale flesh.

"Like a skinned rabbit,"
they tell me, again,

"he was that blue."
I turn my head away.

## MR. HAWTHORNE

Heads huddled close on the hotel
piazza, my husband and the friend
of Franklin Pierce smoke their cigars
and drink the 1820 Schiedam gin.
They talk of Melville, Concord
politics, Alcott's arthritis, and Julian
coming with a fist of maple leaves:
*Look, father, here's a bunch of fire.*

He listens when I speak of the ghost,
turns his burled-chestnut eyes on me
as I tell of the tiny woman's striped
dress, her stockinged feet, her vanishing.

My breasts sting as his gaze leaves me;
milk surges into the cotton pads. He drinks
my apple-toddy, calls me "Miranda,"
borrows my wedding ring, hangs it on string,
and shows my husband how it moves
above the words in a letter, finds hidden
sentiment, angles toward truth.

*Mill House, Artichoke River, West Newbury, 29 November 1854*

## BIRTH (JOHN)

For weeks, I watch the tidal
stream turn the great wheel.

For weeks, I watch the huge
stones grind against each other.

When the pain comes, I am a slat
of paddle pushed into rough

water, or a brown kernel
crushed, spilling its flour.

*Newtonville, Massachusetts, 28 August 1858*

## BIRTH (ROLAND)

This child slides from me
into August heat.
We are slick with sweat:
the doctor in his rumpled
shirt and black wool,
my husband, stooped,
pressing a nervous
hand against my brow,
the nurse whose cheeks
are glazed with it.
Outside, thunder barks,
and as the child slips
from me, the first drops
shake loose and slash
against the glass.

## MR. THAXTER

He clamps his thin lips
shut, retreats to a place
where I cannot follow,

and hunches there, huge
black bird, nothing
but beak and claw.

Flocks of starlings cover
the sky as he wraps himself
in a cloak of sadness

whose thickness gathers
and spreads. He gulps down
misery, bald as any fledgling

that opens its raw throat,
each gesture screaming
"Me, Me, Me."

When I bring him food,
boiled eggs and fingers of toast
laid out neatly on the tray

like soldiers fanned
into regiments, he smashes
each shell, then tumbles

the toast into heaps
of rectangles, his own strict
geometry of loss.

## KARL, AGED EIGHT

As each wave strokes
the hull, he grasps
my skirts and howls.
He limps ashore, dipping
his head toward a shoulder.
He bangs his plate hard,
hard, on the board
until the pieces scatter.
When I beg him to work
on his sewing, he scrunches
next to me, stitches scraps
into rainbow ribbons
swaying between his knees.

## RED

Nine years lace the thicket
around me, barbs of thorn
familiar now and dense, so light
and air no longer reach. I struggle
only in dreams, wake weeping,
touch the red scratches on my skin
as if the wounds were friends.

For nine years I live inside the smallest
of the clutch of Russian dolls, smile
on lacquered face, dot on fevered
cheek—and no giant child near
to pry the wooden oval open.

For nine years I dance the red
gavotte, bow to the line of ribs
and the intransigent pelvis.

*Newtonville, 1861*

## "LAND-LOCKED"

Turning her back on brawling
boys, unemptied chamber pots,
the bolted bedroom door, she
dips her pen in gullible ink:

*Have patience; here are flowers and songs of birds,*
*Beauty and fragrance, wealth of sound and sight,*
*All summer's glory thine from morn till night,*
*And life too full of joy for uttered words.*

She learns to lie, calls it her "little poem."
They pay ten dollars, and she recalls
how last summer Mrs. Bliven said no one
is paid for making a string of shells.

## BONES

Looping twine around
awkward joints, I tie
them to the tree.

In the parlor, I press my face
against cold glass to watch
their pale twirling,

to hear the soft clapping
that patters through my sleep.
Snow falls, and brightness

shrouds twisting femurs of lamb,
ribs of cow—shreds of flesh
cling to them still, tag ends

of fat. In the blue afternoon,
bones sway, jays scream,
and woodpeckers jab

into frozen tissue. As tree
shadows creep across the glare
of snow, I sew trousers for the boys:

—a stitch for every scream of jay
—a stitch for every jab of beak,
—a stitch for every flake on bone.

## BEDTIME STORY

Cinderella chops turnip, scrubs
crusted pots, empties buckets
of ash on the frozen path; a fine
dust blows back on her, grays
her hair, abrades her skin.

The Prince, meanwhile,
is laid out in his glass coffin:
a flutter of breath flowers,
light as hoarfrost, at the rim
of each nostril.

And the three Pigs squeal
as they run through the corridor
the wind makes. Each tiny house
is flimsier than the last—
O, my little pigs, burrow

deep into your straw bedding,
thrust your pink snouts into soft soil,
here's a dream for you—no princes,
no brittle slippers, nothing but
a flank of yielding earth.

*Appledore Island, June–July 1863*

## CIVIL WAR

Around the island, tide
swings its warrant of survival
or destruction, poppies burn
in dazzled frenzy, each flagrant
petal fine enough to catch
her heart and fling it into fire.

In Newtonville he sings Negro
songs with his Harvard cronies,
sleeps till noon, sluices cold
water over head and chest,
shrugs on an unironed shirt,
walks through simmering fields
to Watertown, sits with mother
and sister in the dim coolness
of their mahogany parlor, talks
of Mrs. Cabot, Colonel Shaw's
regiment, the price of strawberries.

She yanks weeds from roots
of peonies, sprinkles lime
at the plot's edge.

In Georgia Colonel Shaw
writes to his wife:
*Tomorrow is Sunday,*
*and perhaps you will be*
*at Staten Island; . . . but wherever*

*you are I wish I could go to church*
*with you, and saunter about*
*in some pretty garden*
*afterwards.*

        .   .   .

A wall six feet high

of amputated legs

Don't move      he shouts

No      she cries

Now

No

        .   .   .

I fill pepper boxes with poison
                  hellebore for thrips
                  sulphur for mildew
                  yellow snuff for aphids
                  cayenne pepper
                  kerosene emulsion
                  whale-oil soap
*In the ditch they lay piled*
*negroes & whites*
*four & five deep*
*on each other*
*there could not have been*

*less than 250 in the moat*
*some partially submerged*

He dabs a starched napkin
to his lip, smoothes strands
of hair across the bald spot,
complains about the heat.

"You are missed in Newtonville,"
he writes. "John & Lony
miss you too."

Her spade cuts clean
through twisted rhubarb roots,
each stalk pale at the base;
its heavy leaves can kill.

They stamp on the bodies,
push them in the trench,
wrap scarves around mouths,
try not to breathe, powder
clings to boots, clumps
in the folds of trousers.

He curls in his bed, face
to the wall, old habit.

•   •   •

*Where are you?*

Water slaps rock,
the amputee unleashes

a curse, cream spills
from its silver pitcher

*How did you get here?*

Dropped thread, birds gobbled
crumbs, moss on each side,
each tree, glass compass
splintered in my tight fist

*bone*

# 1863 BODIES

Tom Thumb and his bride
(two feet, eight inches tall) stand

on the polished top of a grand
piano to greet their guests.

In Richmond, men riot
over bread.

Gettysburg's streets are black
with bundled bodies, prowling dogs.

In New York City, mobs attack
the Colored Orphan Asylum,

and, finding the orphans gone, kill
whomsoever they can.

In England, thirty thousand
die of scarlet fever.

In Ireland, once again,
potatoes rot.

And in Paris, a painting
of a naked woman, picnicking

with two clothed men,
can somehow shock.

## MRS. THAXTER

The bird's skull is light—
tucks between the eyesockets,
like the folds of a dress
hanging in a closet far
from the body's turbulence.

I keep it on my desk, next
to the inkwell, and touch it often:
the long extended beak that pushes
forward like the prow of a ship,
triangles formed by bone bridges
supporting the chamber that once
held the brain, looped with oval
entrances for nerves; the slight
depression, a gentle mark
like an infant's fontanel,
where the skull begins its slope
back to the life that pulses
out of reach of the fierce eyes.

I touch that fierceness, make it mine—
that smooth essential purpose,
each cell bent on survival.

When the world greets me,
it sees a white dress, a dewy rose
pinned on the breast. No one
sees this skull, this bone
bridge across which I walk.

*Appledore Island, February 1866*

## DEATHBED (THOMAS LAIGHTON)

I shut my mind to the image
of him, paralytic, in the wind-
chilled house, until Cedric writes:
"Someone has to sit up every night."

I bring the rum and brandy
they requested, purple bottles
of lobelia to damp the pain.

He does not know me, begs
me to send for Celia.

I bathe the spongy legs,
spread salve on crusting sores,
and dream he is a thin heron,
turned from me, beating
its way through air, absorbed
in the long flight.

## MR. DICKENS

He sits beside me at the formal
dinner, beneath the candelabrum
brought from Rome, leans

close as I tell of the Shoals,
the wreck of the *Sagunto*,
the midwife and her boat.

He has been so weak he could
only sip the liquids Annie brought
—cream, rum, champagne.

With plump fingers, he touches
my shell necklace, swears he feels
the salt breeze on his cheek.

Beneath the table, his swollen
foot throbs in the black silk
pouch made by Annie's hands.

# THE SMUTTYNOSE MURDERS

I rub arnica on the frozen feet
of the one who survives, and scribble
notes for the *Atlantic Monthly*.

On the white ground, red
tracks surround the house.

No one touches the bodies.
Nightgowns flutter high
around waists, pleated
tucks lead only into red.

One slumps under a bed—
she had her teeth pulled,
five days ago, by a Portsmouth
dentist. Above her nose, bone
surges through the bright
lips of the wound.

The other rests close
to the stove: ears dangle
from thin flaps
where the axe sliced
through coils of hair.

When the coroner's men
leave, the women bathe

and clothe the bodies:
a wedding dress, a skirt
of black moiré, gray
silk blouse, velvet
at the neck.

## DEATHBED (ELIZA LAIGHTON)

The whale body is beached, held
in heavy sheets. I feed it,
wash it, roll it on its side to wipe.
While it sleeps, I paint and lose myself
in my "little landscapes."
Over a hundred china pieces: calm
olive branches, lizards, pansies,
grass; a Japanese lady smiles
from the center of each sea-green
plate. I write to Annie of my struggle
with the human figure: "I know
it will be difficult, but I think
it can be done, that delicate work
of copying the face and hands
and arms." While I hold
my hand steady, hers quivers.

*Appledore Island, September 1879*

## MR. HUNT

He fears to leave the island, dreads the train's
cinders and the wild screeching of the wheels.
He sits on the piazza, eyes closed, as Mr. Thaxter
speaks of the Albany murals, Hunt on his high
ladder, paint brushes gripped, the twelve-foot
Columbus soaring above, with Fortune, Faith,
and Science at his side. He shudders at each
mention of the cinders. Mr. Thaxter reads
him Browning: *she rose and from her form*
*Withdrew the dripping cloak and shawl.*
I find the body, face down, in the pond behind
the hotel. It turns slowly, and the wind flutters
one sleeve, like a passenger's hand flickering
at a window as the train builds speed.

*148 Charles Street, Boston, 23 April 1881*

## MR. FIELDS

Behind tall windows, a silhouette
of elm, a slate river. On the low table,
bone china cups, and plates of buttered
scones. When he falls, Annie and I
drag him to his chair and heave him
into it. He grabs my hand, presses
so strongly the fingers lose all feeling.
Impassive busts gaze down. I hold
the book and Annie reads to him
from Matthew Arnold, her voice
a cool gray river that ferries him away.

*Boston, March 1884*

## THE EICHBERGS' RECEPTION

In the back parlor, pruned of piano
and music stands, I weave lilies
and roses into exotic swags. After Weber

and his crew lay out the scalloped lace,
serving spoons, bags of sugared almonds,
he leads me to the cellar to applaud

his masterpiece. Wrapped in ice and burlap,
the ice-cream swan swims on a bed of melon
carved into waves that rush outward as if

the bird had plopped down vertically
into a green pond. Eye a dusky grape,
beak a wedge of painted cardboard,

wings of ludicrous frills. Weber claims
it signifies "innocence and virtue." To me,
the plump eye winks seduction and escape.

## DEATHBED (LEVI LINCOLN THAXTER)

They let her visit his deathbed
only when they choose.

He has a sister and a son to wait
on him now, no need of wife.

On the last day, having ceased
the screaming and the thrashing,

he lies still. She looks down
at the yellow flesh, the sheet

drawn over the belly, hiding
the heat of the infection.

She touches the harpstring
of rib, fluted and clean,

naked without its flesh.
She softens as he hardens.

Nothing remains to forgive. Hour
by hour, he is becoming bone.

*shell*

## IN THE DREAM

The statues were draped
in snow, granite pedestals

dissolved in billowing
drifts, and the fierce-beaked

public men had become waves
that crested and did not break.

On a bench in the Public
Garden, I sat wrapped

in mourning, a thick black
speck on an unwritten page.

Under the pond's eiderdown,
unseen ice; under the ice,

flickers almost obliterated;
deeper still, frogs swaddled

numb in layers of mud,
summer locked in each tight

throat. Into that silence
leapt a gunshot crack of ice.

## BOSTON 1884

I embrace it all: the fifteen-thousand-dollar bed
of tulips under the hooves of Washington's stone

horse, Irish servants impossible to train, thin
arms that dangle from the windows of the Charles

Street Jail, mansard roofs and bulbous domes,
gray crusted shells of oysters on crushed ice, pale

ghosts of magnolia, raised purple scars and sleeves
pinned at the elbow, the forty-five hundred wooden

piles that hold up Trinity, incandescent lamps
in the chandeliers of Hotel Vendôme, the gloss

on the swan's wing around the pedaling boy,
mounds of manure steaming a benediction.

*Appledore Island, August 1884*

## NIGHT HAMMOCK

Canvas at my back,
Cygnus above me

stretching out a taut
extravagant neck—

between two deaths
I have space

enough
for swinging.

*Boston, December 1884*

## SÉANCE

Hesitant, they creep closer,
shreds of mist pulling trains
of icy air through the cavern
of the room. While Pinny's setter
rubs his snout against her knee
and growls, Mrs. Darrah raises
her long nose to greet them.
Annie's fingers tense in mine,
her rings digging into my palm
as I feel an outline of a hand
settle on my scalp. Something
tentative and gentle brushes
against my cheek, like flakes
of snow sliding from a sill.

*Appledore Island, August 1887*

## GIRL

Past racks of cloud strung
      over Appledore, past barnacles
that cling and thicken, past thirty
      years of bitterness, brine washing
round my heart, past flattering chatter,
      hypocrisies lush as weed on harbor rock,
I'll seek her till I find her standing there,
      blinking upward at the man, ignorant
of what they'll both endure. I want to tell
      her she is less than she thinks, and more.
I want to show her how water licks rock
      persistently, wearing it down, making
the islands smaller; and how water streams
      its relentless grace around her feet.

*Boston, 1888*

## COMPANIONS

If, as glossy-haired Mohini claims,
loss is the companion of joy

(I see them sitting placidly together
on a bench in Louisburg Square,

early September, an eager leaf detaches
from the elm above their heads, and swaying

as it floats, half buoyed by an errant draft
of air, lands on Joy's shoulder, as she turns

to Loss and asks about his nephews—
little Grief and baby Worry),

*if* loss is the companion of joy,
must not joy then be the companion of loss?

He turns to her, touches her gloved
hand, remarks on the angle of the sun,

the frost he saw, like lace,
on the morning lawn.

## MORPHINE

This tide foams wide and full
as poppy petals: each new
and rippled plane glides
shining on the last, dissolves
in a shimmer, tumbles
on rock and drenches
a nothingness that drags,
hauls, spins, slow,
slow, in circuits old
as a planet's wobbled dance.

O, bring me needles,
ampoules, powder
ground by pestle
on striated marble.

Fetch me the seagull's
skull, mask from a Venetian
alley, beak arcing white
into darkness, for this last
carnival. The grave
flesh melts. What's left
is light as bone.

## SPIRIT

Later they will say I died
like Goethe,
asking for light.
I did ask Minna to pull

the curtain so that light
would wake me,
but my last request
was a soft boiled egg,

which they will edit
out of the myth.
I want to tell them
to leave the egg in,

to let it sit there,
in its wooden cup—
at the center of a darkening
room, the gleam

of bone-white shell.

*notes*

# NOTES

The story that is usually told is simple and dramatic.

In 1839, when Celia Laighton was four years old, her father, Thomas Laighton, took the post of lighthouse keeper at White Island, one of the Isles of Shoals, ten miles off Portsmouth, New Hampshire. He moved his family (wife Eliza, daughter Celia, and infant son Oscar) from the bustling streets of Portsmouth to a stone cottage on the tiny rocky island: "our storm-swept bit of rock," as Oscar would later describe it. A third child, Cedric, was born the following year.

During her twelfth year, Celia Laighton was courted by Levi Thaxter: Harvard graduate, lawyer, partner with her father in the construction of the grand Appledore House, and tutor to the three Laighton children. At age sixteen, she married him. After several years, during which the couple found lodging with gracious friends and relatives, they settled in a house bought for them by the Thaxter parents, in Newtonville, outside of Boston. The marriage—which yielded three children, the eldest of whom, Karl, was said to have suffered brain damage at birth—proved painfully unhappy.

Escaping the misery of this marriage, Thaxter constructed a new identity, that of writer, and artist. She became friendly with most of the prominent New England literati and artists (Nathaniel Hawthorne, John Greenleaf Whittier, James and Annie Fields, Sarah Orne Jewett, Oliver Wendell Holmes, Harriet Beecher Stowe, Childe Hassam, and William Morris Hunt, among others) and a few international stars (Charles Dickens, Robert Browning). In 1861 her first published poem, "Land-locked," appeared in the *Atlantic Monthly* and launched a career of poetry and nonfiction writing

(*Among the Isles of Shoals, An Island Garden*). Under the tutelage of Ross Sterling Turner and Childe Hassam, she also gained some painting expertise; and from the 1870s onward, her income was supplemented by the sale of painted cups, tiles, bowls, and delicate hand-illustrated volumes of her poems. During the summer season, writers, musicians, and artists would flock to the fashionable Appledore House, spending mornings and evenings in Thaxter's cottage, listening to Chopin nocturnes and breathing the perfume of the amassed flowers picked fresh from her garden. For those who know the Hassam paintings of her garden, she seems to stand eternally there, head bent, touching a flower—the epitome of an unlettered, untutored artist, in tune with the natural world.

She died on Appledore Island in August 1894. Childe Hassam and J. Appleton Brown, a fellow artist, arranged a bier of bayberry around the corpse, which was laid out in the parlor of her cottage, and both acted as pallbearers, helping to carry the coffin to the flower-filled grave.

On Appledore today, in the quiet family cemetery, four stone walls enclose the simple markers: Mother, Father, Celia, Oscar, Cedric.

• • •

But there may be another story.

Myths and new identities don't just happen. Most likely, for Thaxter, they were formed out of a will and a necessity as hard as the granite that builds the Isles of Shoals. As she wrote in relation to her painting, "I know I can do it, and I will do it." It is clear that she worked whatever connections were available in order to amass such an extensive list of famous friends. She smiled and laughed and cajoled—and kept the pain of her marriage a private matter, shared only with a friend as intimate as Annie Fields. She consistently edited out details of her education, presenting herself as more unlettered than she actually was. She dramatized herself as a simple island creature, making buttons out of shells and wearing shell necklaces. She wore antique dresses of white, black, or gray. And while she complained about being called the "rose of the isles," each day she wore a single rose pinned to her dress.

Her public persona was also shaped by the period. Her market determined the writing. Due to her husband's refusal, or psychological inability, to work, she was always in need of money, and she wrote to earn it. As a consequence, she lacked the freedom, which Emily Dickinson contrived, to write what she pleased; and one of the great ironies of Thaxter's career is that her first published poem may be her best. Particularly in her poems, she delivers the pious and sentimental messages that her audience expected; yet we can see from her nonfiction that she possessed a wild sense of humor and a gusto for the gothic (for example, her *Atlantic Monthly* account of the Smuttynose murders of 1873), features that remind one more of Margaret Atwood than of Thaxter's contemporaries. A note of harsh practicality often sounds, and the vision can be unsparingly bleak.

Imagination and history partner each other in this work. While *Becoming Bone* claims no definitive truth, it offers new insight into the life of a remarkable and complex woman.

. . .

p. 7, "News": Oscar is Celia's young brother.

p. 8, "Thaw": "Swathed in warm fog" is a direct quotation from Thaxter's prose work *Among the Isles of Shoals*.

p. 11, "Whale-Oil": Lunging (originally Londoner's) is the island closest to White Island.

p. 12, "Midwife": Gosport was the village on Star Island.

p. 13, "Childbed": This is the only place where I have knowingly detoured from the historical record: Cedric was born in Portsmouth, not on White Island.

p. 17, "Mirage": The "Harvard man" is Levi Thaxter, who had come out to the islands for the sake of his health after suffering a psychological crisis brought on by the refusal of his family to allow him a career on the stage. They wanted him to practice law, for which he had been trained.

p. 18, "The Harvard Man": The quotation comes from Robert Browning's "Soliloquy of the Spanish Cloister." Levi Thaxter was obsessed with Browning; late in his life, he gave public readings of Browning.

p. 21, "Appledore House": This huge and fashionable hotel was built on Appledore Island (formerly Hog Island) by Thomas Laighton and Levi Thaxter. Nathaniel Hawthorne describes it: "a large building, with a piazza or promenade before, about 120 feet in length, or more. Yes; it must be more. It is a central edifice of upwards of 70 feet, with two wings. At one end of the promenade is a covered verandah, thirty or forty feet square, so situated that the breeze draws across it . . . and it is the breeziest and comfortablest place in the world, on a hot day."

p. 22, "Tutor": Celia Laighton copied out the "George Washington" and "Fame" quotations as a handwriting exercise.

p. 26, "Memory": Thomas Laighton's journal includes the terse 20 January 1849 entry: "killed heifer belonging to T, and self—sent him half." This moment marked the dissolution of their bitter partnership.

p. 29, "Wedding": Jonas is Levi's brother. The Thaxter parents did not attend.

p. 30, "Marriage Bed": Before setting sail for Troy, Paris and Helen consummated their love on the island of Marathonisi.

p. 36, "Song": The setting is a cottage close to the Appledore House hotel.

p. 38, "Mr. Hawthorne": Hawthorne records his visit to Appledore House and his friendship with Levi Thaxter in his *American Notebooks*, entries from 30 August to 16 September 1852. "Miranda" is Prospero's daughter, who knows nothing but her island, in Shakespeare's *The Tempest*.

p. 41, "Mr. Thaxter": Levi Thaxter apparently suffered from severe bouts of depression.

p. 44, "Land-locked": "Land-locked" is the title of Thaxter's first published poem, submitted by a friend or relative to the *Atlantic Monthly*, where James Russell Lowell accepted it and provided the title. The poem was published anonymously. Mrs. Bliven was a summer guest at the Appledore House.

p. 47, "Civil War": Col. Robert Gould Shaw commanded the 54th Massachusetts Regiment, the famous Negro regiment that fought at the battle of Fort Wagner on 18 July 1863. The excerpt from his letter and the description of the bodies at Fort Wagner come from *Blue-Eyed Child of Fortune: the Civil War Letters of Robert Gould Shaw*, ed. Russell Duncan (Athens: University of Georgia Press, 1999). "Lony" is the family's pet name for Roland. By this time, the pattern was established of Celia Thaxter taking care of Karl, and Levi Thaxter taking care of the two younger boys.

p. 53, "1863 Bodies": The riots in New York resulted from the

1863 draft. The painting in the final stanza is Manet's *Déjeuner sur l'herbe.*

p. 56, "Mr. Dickens": The setting is the house of James and Annie Fields (Thaxter's closest friend). 148 Charles Street was Dickens's base during his American readings tour. During his stay, Dickens suffered from gout. He and Annie Fields would spend flirtatious mornings playing with her new sewing machine, hence the black silk pouch. The morning after the dinner, Dickens told his hostess that Mrs. Thaxter's stories had taken such a hold of him that he woke in the night, thinking of her. The *Sagunto* was a Spanish ship wrecked on Smuttynose Island in 1813.

p. 57, "The Smuttynose Murders": The 1873 Smuttynose murders led to a famous nineteenth-century legal case. Thaxter knew one of the victims personally: Karen Hontvet had worked for the Laighton family until a few weeks before her death.

p. 59, "Deathbed (Eliza Laighton)": During Eliza Laighton's long decline, Thaxter and Karl would remain on Appledore Island during the winter, rather than returning to Newtonville.

p. 60, "Mr. Hunt": William Morris Hunt, the famous painter, arrived at Appledore exhausted and depressed. It is likely that his drowning was a suicide. The quotation comes from Robert Browning's "Porphyria's Lover."

p. 62, "The Eichbergs' Reception": Julius Eichberg, famous violinist and composer, was a good friend of Thaxter's. The poem's occasion is the preparation for his daughter's wedding reception.

p. 63, "Deathbed (Levi Lincoln Thaxter)": During his final illness, Levi Thaxter stayed at his sister Lucy's house in Watertown, where he was nursed by his youngest son, Roland. The final diagnosis was "chronic peritonitis."

p. 68, "Boston 1884": Trinity is Trinity Church. The pedaling boy still propels the Swan Boat in the Public Garden.

p. 70, "Séance": Rose Darrah, a well known Boston medium, convinced Thaxter—and half-convinced her friends Annie Fields and Sarah Orne Jewett (Pinny)—of the possibility of communication with the dead. Darrah was later revealed as a charlatan.

p. 72, "Companions": Mohini Mohum Chatterjee, former devotee of Madame Blavatsky, took Boston by storm in the late 1880s and made a particularly strong impression on Thaxter, helping her toward a religion that mixed Christianity with eastern thought.

p. 73, "Morphine": From 1890 until her death in 1894, Thaxter suffered severe heart problems. Initially she attempted her own treatment; later her physician prescribed champagne. In 1893 she had two surgeries for skin cancer. Finally, morphine was used to control the pain.

p. 74, "Spirit": Minna is Thaxter's maid.